BRITAIN IN OLD PHOTOGRAPHS

LITERARY OXFORD

NANCY HOOD

SUTTON PUBLISHING LIMITED

Sutton Publishing Limited
Phoenix Mill · Thrupp · Stroud
Gloucestershire · GL5 2BU

XFORDSHIRE BOOKS

First published 1999

Title page: Bird's eye view of Oxford, *c.* 1890, looking up a traffic-free High Street towards Carfax from Magdalen Tower.

British Library Cataloguing in Publication Data
A catalogue record for this book is available from the British Library.

ISBN 0-7509-2115-3

Typeset in 10.5/13.5 Photina.
Typesetting and origination by
Sutton Publishing Limited.
Printed in Great Britain by
Ebenezer Baylis, Worcester.

CONTENTS

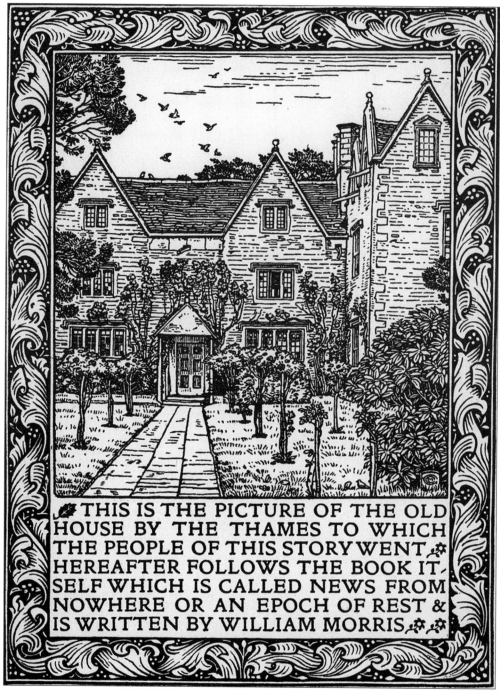

THIS IS THE PICTURE OF THE OLD
HOUSE BY THE THAMES TO WHICH
THE PEOPLE OF THIS STORY WENT.
HEREAFTER FOLLOWS THE BOOK IT-
SELF WHICH IS CALLED NEWS FROM
NOWHERE OR AN EPOCH OF REST &
IS WRITTEN BY WILLIAM MORRIS.

William Morris's woodcut of Kelmscott Manor in Oxfordshire, which he used as the frontispiece for the Kelmscott Press edition of *News from Nowhere*, 1891. The house was meant to represent a Utopian way of life, drawing on the best of the past together with current social ideals.

INTRODUCTION

Oxford has figured in literature and in literary life since its name *Oxnaforda*, later *Oxenforde*, was first mentioned in the Anglo Saxon Chronicle in the early years of the tenth century, as King Edward occupied both London and Oxford against the Mercians. The settlement had grown up at the ford across the Thames, on the important route between Mercia and Wessex, and at the gates of a convent founded in the eighth century by the princess Frideswide. Her heroic story entwines the rivalries of the kingdoms of Mercia and Wessex, as the Saxon princess refuses to be wed to the Mercian prince, seeks refuge at Binsey, sees her pursuer blinded by lightning, but cures him with holy water; he leaves her in peace, a better and more humble man, while she carries out her vow to remain a virgin and found a convent. These legendary origins of Oxford, buried in myth, but slowly being revealed through archaeology as having the germ of truth, have made their contribution to the magic and mystery of the place, its *genius loci*, so often alluded to in literature from Chaucer to Lewis Carroll.

By Chaucer's time (1343–1400), the University was well established, and the 'clerke of Oxenforde' was a character in the *Canterbury Tales* which could be recognised by that varied audience of pilgrims. The clerk in 'The Miller's Tale', who lodges with a carpenter of Osney, is innocent, charming and clever; he seduces the miller's beautiful wife, has a close shave, escapes using his wits, and provides a model for the romance of student life at Oxford for centuries.

The tension between 'town and gown' had already erupted in the St Scholastica Day riot and massacre of many students in 1355, and left another legacy from the middle ages – the University as the cuckoo in the nest. Issues such as student pranks, wild behaviour, town lodgings, local girls and unpaid debts have remained to be grappled with, and have been story-fodder for writers from and about Oxford ever since.

But the magic of Oxford is enough to attract writers as visitors, to see the spires, to talk with like minds, to dine, to study, to observe, to describe, to criticise, or just to be, among them Shakespeare, William Camden, who called Oxford 'our most noble Athens', Celia Fiennes, Alexander Pope, William Cobbett, Dr Samuel Johnson, George Eliot and Jane Austen. The view from the surrounding hills has always inspired and thrilled, and figured in descriptions, paintings, prints and photographs.

For many authors, the coming of age, the passing through the University, the years spent or mis-spent, the friends who reappear throughout life in a 'Dance to the

Balliol dons in the Fellows Garden, *c.* 1890; the Master, D. Caird, elected in 1893, is the venerable gentleman second from left.

Music of Time' provided the subject of the first novel and launched many a career, from John Aubrey to John Betjeman. Others have simply used the setting, the privileged, cloistered life, the remoteness from ordinary folk, as a backdrop – the Oxford novel and the Oxford detective story number in hundreds.

To give a flavour of how Oxford looked to the writers in their time here, to set the scene for some of the action in their lives and books, are the aims of this choice of photographs. I hope they give another dimension to your stroll around Oxford and your trips in the county, for these ruins are indeed inhabited and these stones have stories to tell.

CHAPTER ONE

COLLEGE HAUNTS &
TOWN PLEASURES

Above the clatter of 3 Cornmarket, formerly the Crown Inn, the Painted Room survives, covered in warm Elizabethan pattern and colour – you can almost smell the log fires. Shakespeare stayed here once a year when he was en route between London and Stratford. He was godfather to William D'Avenant, the son of the innkeeper, and according to gossip at the time perhaps even his natural father. William D'Avenant (1606–68, and undergraduate at Lincoln in the 1620s) was also a playwright and poet: he introduced scenery on to the stage for his plays, and tried his hand at opera. John Aubrey gives this account in *Brief Lives*: 'he wrote with the very spirit that Shakespeare [wrote] and seemed contented enough to be thought his son: he would tell then the story as above, in which way his mother had a very light report.' His mother was said to be very beautiful and quick-witted.

The wall paintings of 3 Cornmarket were restored in 1927, and the room is open by appointment through Oxford City Council.

Next door to the Crown, another rarity – the coaching inn of the Cross, now the Golden Cross, where Alexander Pope stayed in 1735. The fifteenth-century north range is now shops with *Pizza Express* above; original timberwork and wall paintings were revealed during restoration and conversion to the restaurant.

The Golden Cross's gateway opens on to Cornmarket. This photograph of 1907 could almost have been taken in Pope's time.

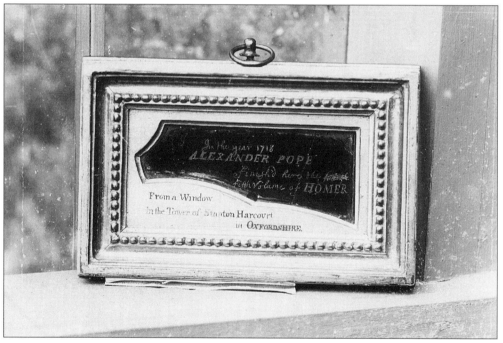

Alexander Pope passed through the county often and stayed in Stanton Harcourt, in the fifteenth-century tower that was a remnant of the former manor house. Here he worked on *The Iliad*, but who recorded this on the glass window taken from the tower? This souvenir is known to have been in Nuneham Courtenay, the Harcourt's other great estate on the Thames near Abingdon.

The tower is now known as Pope's Tower. It can be visited when the grounds and gardens are open to the public.

Another port of call for Pope was Rousham. The literary connections of this gothicky fantasy of a mansion also included Gay and Horace Walpole, all visitors to the Cottrell-Dormer family of Rousham. Pope's patron, Mrs Caesar, left her collection of books, letters and portraits to her daughter, who married into the family. These can be seen there when the house is open. Rousham House was remodelled by William Kent in 1738–40, with a gothic façade added to the seventeenth-century gabled manor house to blend in with the newly landscaped grounds, creating what Pevsner describes as 'an early Tudor palace in free Gothic style, often confused with classical detail'.

Portraits of the Cottrell-Dormer family, of the Caesars and of Pope, along with the letters and library, form an outstanding collection of literary gems at Rousham.

The William Kent-landscaped grounds are a milestone in classical-to-romantic English country house garden design. Temples, grottoes, springs, statues and mythological allusions create a suitably inspiring environment for the work of Pope translating the classics and the appreciation of Walpole, whose own gothicised fantasy Strawberry Hill is even more extravagant than Rousham. This is the Long Bridge over the Cherwell, which runs through the Park.

Thomas Hearne, the antiquary, suffered from the University's conformist stance on religious and political correctness in the turbulent generation following the Civil War. He took his degree from 1699 to 1703, and through his post as Keeper of the Bodleian Library indulged his antiquarian and medieval textual interests, publishing the collections. But as a Jacobite he lost the post. His tombstone is the one on the lower right, in the churchyard of St Peter in the East, seen here in 1909. It has now been converted to become the library of St Edmund Hall adjacent to it, and where Hearne lodged as an undergraduate.

The classical scholar and poet Joseph Addison, Fellow of Magdalen College from 1698 to 1711, regularly followed his favourite walk around the College grounds along the Cherwell and past the Mill. It was known as the Water Walk, but now it is called Addison's Walk after him.

Generations of both scholars and local people have followed it, searching for inspiration, or simply to admire the winter to spring display of wild flowers, and the highlight of snakeshead fritillaries covering the meadow in May.

Dr Samuel Johnson had the rooms on the second floor over the gateway of Pembroke College when he came up in 1728. The College is seen here in a photograph of 1890, after the seventeenth-century building was remodelled to look more Gothic. However, he was forced to abandon his studies before he was halfway through because of poverty – thus the award of MA on the publication of the Dictionary in 1755 was a special achievement. He revisited Oxford many times, dining with Boswell and academics at University College, drinking tea and making conversation at Christ Church and with his friend Thomas Warton, editor of the *Oxford Sausage*, in Trinity. He thought tutorials the best manner of teaching, and that lectures would eventually be replaced by print!

The Codrington Library of All Souls College owes its foundation to the bequest of Christopher Codrington, a Fellow, in 1690, but with a fortune from sugar plantations in Barbados and Antigua. The celebrated building is by Hawksmoor and was begun in 1716, but the sundial (below), which was previously in the front quad over the chapel, dates from 1658, and was probably designed by Sir Christopher Wren, Bursar of the College at that time. In the print above it looks as if it was used as a long gallery for promenading Fellows' visitors at a time when the University was known for good living and little learning, rather than a hallowed hall of academic study. The classical interior, complete with the statue of Codrington as Governor of Barbados in Roman dress, is clothed in a Gothic exterior to match the medieval chapel of the College on the other side of the quad.

Here also T.E. Lawrence, 'Lawrence of Arabia', was a Fellow, and began *The Seven Pillars of Wisdom*, in 1926. The College has a small collection of relics and a pencil-drawn portrait. The photograph of the Great Quad dates from Warden Adam's tenure, 1933–45, with a tennis court marked out on the superbly tended grass: the College has no undergraduates and no playing fields.

Lawrence lived at 2 Polstead Road until 1926.

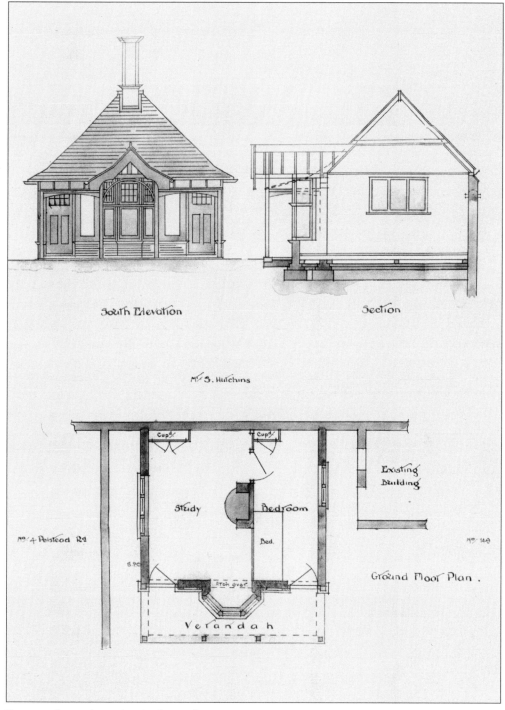

South Elevation   Section

Mrs S. Hutchins

Study   Bedroom

Existing Building

No 4 Poistead Rd   No 40

Ground Floor Plan.

Verandah

He wrote from a bungalow in the garden.

This monument to Percy Bysshe Shelley (1792–1822) in University College is a rather late tribute to the poet who was sent down from the University after only one year for suspected authorship of a pamphlet entitled *The Necessity of Atheism*. Shelley refused to admit to it as a matter of principle; the University authorities, firmly clerical, Anglican and conformist, expelled him and his friend Thomas Hogg who complained on his behalf.

Shelley had been set to enjoy Oxford to the full: conducting chemical experiments in his rooms; roaming over Shotover Hill reading poetry and practising with his pistol; avoiding lectures and 'sporting the oak' (or working in his rooms with both doors closed, a signal not to be disturbed) all part of the search for the meaning of life by a young man.

The monument, intended for his tomb at the Protestant Cemetery in Rome, shows the drowned poet in marble relief being mourned by the muse of poetry, and was set up in the college in 1893.

Henry James, the American author and Anglophile, writes of Oxford in *Portraits of Places*, and a number of colleges and their gardens appear in the stories in *A Passionate Pilgrim*. He lived for a time, in 1894, at 15 Beaumont Street, which is on the corner opposite St John's Street, on the shady side, looking towards Worcester College. Beaumont Street was laid out on the site of medieval Beaumont Palace in 1828–37, and is seen here in its nearly original style. The one bay of the Ashmolean Museum on the right dates from 1841–5; the Playhouse has not yet been built; and the Randolph Hotel is out of the picture.

Some college gardens that featured in the stories, from around this period, were photographed by Taunt. This is Wadham in 1870.

W.B. Yeats spent some years in the city and nearby. He lived here at 5 Broad Street, opposite Balliol College from 1919 to 1921; this pair was demolished in the 1920s. He and his family then rented Minchen's Cottage in Shillingford, on Warborough Road, and later Cuttlebrook House, 42 High Street in Thame. While living in London, Yeats had been acquainted with William Morris and the pre-Raphaelites, and also Oscar Wilde; while in Oxford he was among the writers entertained at Garsington Manor by Lady Ottoline Morrell.

CHAPTER TWO

CITY OF DREAMS & LOST CAUSES:
MATTHEW ARNOLD

Matthew Arnold, as an undergraduate from 1841 to 1843, would have seen these Balliol buildings when he came up to read classics, not the Victorian façades of Broad Street and St Giles we see today.

He took a fellowship at Oriel after his degree, and a post as school inspector allowed him time to write poetry, essays and criticism. He was elected Professor of Poetry in 1857. Almost single-handedly, in his poems and criticism, he crystallised the world's image of Oxford as the city of dreaming spires, the home of lost causes, and the haunt of 'The Scholar Gypsy'.

Like many undergraduates Matthew Arnold spent a good deal of time rambling the ridge of hills which encircle the city, boating on the river and frequenting country public houses from Wytham to Beckley. His good friend Arthur Hugh Clough was a constant companion, and the memories of those youthful excursions were rendered poignant, even romantic, by his early death. Sadness and nostalgia for past pleasures, youth, friendship and innocence are always near the surface of the poetry, and are themes of 'The Scholar Gypsy' and 'Thyrsis', his elegy to Clough.

'The Scholar Gypsy' was a seventeenth-century tale by Joseph Glanvill (Exeter College, 1655) of the youthful scholar who abandoned the discipline of established learning and sought true knowledge from nature and the lore of gypsy travellers. He is seen, briefly, shadowy, at all the familiar places, just for a moment before disappearing, still searching: 'And came, as most men deem'd to little good'.

The ferry at Bablock Hythe, one of the crossing places of the Thames below Cumnor.

Thee at the ferry Oxford riders blithe,
Returning home on summer-nights, have met
Crossing the stripling Thames at Bab-lock hithe,
Trailing in the cool stream thy fingers wet,
As the punt's rope chops round;
And leaning backward in a pensive dream,
And fostering in thy lap a heap of flowers
Pluck'd in shy fields and distant Wychwood bowers,
And thine eyes resting on the moonlit stream,

And then they land, and thou art seen no more! –
Maidens, who from the distant hamlets come
To dance around the Fyfield elm in May,
Oft through the darkening fields have seen thee roam,
Or cross a stile into the public way.
Oft thou hast given them store
Of flowers – the frail-leaf'd, white anemony,
Dark blue bells drench'd with dews of summer eves,
And purple orchises with spotted leaves –
But none hath words she can report of thee.

The single elm tree on the ridge at Boars Hill.

From 'Thyrsis'
Runs it not here, the track by Childsworth Farm,
Past the high wood, to where the elm-tree crowns
The hill behind whose ridge the sunset flames?
The signal-elm, that looks on Ilsley Downs
The Vale, the three lone weirs, the youthful Thames? .
We prized it dearly; while it stood, we said,
Our friend, the Gipsy Scholar, was not dead;
While the tree lived, he in these fields lived on.

The famous view from Hinksey Hill.

And that sweet city with her dreaming spires,
She needs not June for beauty's heightening,
Lovely all times she lies, lovely tonight!

CHAPTER THREE

BALLIOL MEN

Gerard Manley Hopkins kept a diary of his time at Balliol in the 1860s, when he taught both Benjamin Jowett an
Matthew Arnold. He too spent time enjoying the countryside around, and reflected on the changing appearance o
1870s Oxford in his poem 'Duns Scotus's Oxford':

> Towery city and branchy between towers;
> Cukoo-echoing, bell-swarmed, lark-charmed,
> rook-racked, river-rounded. . . .

but then:

> Thou hast a base and brickish skirt there, sours
> That neighbour nature thy grey beauty is grounded
> Best in; graceless growth, . . .

This referred to the worker and artisan houses in Jericho, east, south and west Oxford which were hurriedly buil
for the army of employees in the breweries, printing presses, tailors, the ironworks, quarries, and of course th
university and college servants, in the growing town.

He might have seen this view from one of Balliol's towers, to inspire those lines.

The new buildings of Balliol were impressive and imposing, solid and worthy to the Victorian eye.

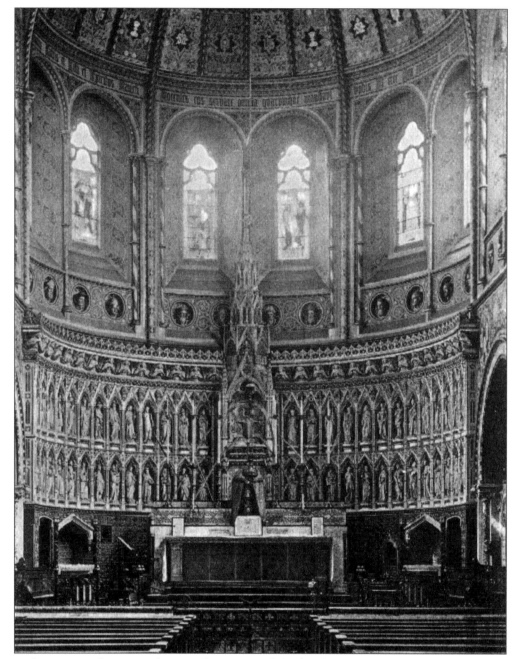

As the curate at the new Gothic revival, Roman Catholic, St Aloysius' Church on Woodstock Road, the interior of which is seen here in about 1905, Hopkins returned to Oxford in 1878. The poem 'Binsey Poplars' was written when the trees along the river were cut down, in another example of the defiling of the 'neighbour nature', or spirit of the place.

> O if we but knew what we do
> When we delve or hew
> Hack and rack the growing green!
> Since country is so tender. . . .

The quiet corner of Binsey, protected from the Oxford sprawl by the river flood plain.

Another Balliol man, from 1869 to 1872, Professor of Poetry and Shakespearian critic, was A.C. Bradley. He is buried in St Cross churchyard, as is Kenneth Grahame, author of *The Wind in the Willows*, and Charles Williams, one of the Inklings. Kenneth Grahame's son is buried with him; there is an epitaph by Anthony Hope Hawkins. A memorial window to Grahame is in the chapel of St Edward's School, where he was in one of the first classes in the new school buildings on Woodstock Road (1868–75). Kenneth Grahame lived in a Tudor farmhouse, Bohams, in Blewbury not far away, and called the area 'King Alfred's country'. Walter Pater, another student of Jowett and Arnold, and influential writer among the intellectuals of the age, is also buried here.

The little St Cross Church figures in Dorothy L. Sayers' novel *Busman's Honeymoon*.

The fine Gothic Revival buildings of St Edward's School on Woodstock Road. A stream of writers emanated from the 'branchy towers' and intellectual hothouse of Balliol in this period: Algernon Swinburne, Hilaire Belloc, C.E Montague, L.P. Hartley, Nevil Shute, Arnold Toynbee, Cyril Connolly.

Aldous Huxley, at Balliol from 1913 to 1916, drew on his experiences at college, and afterwards as a guest of the Haldanes in North Oxford and at Garsington Manor staying with the Morrells, in his novels, particularly *Eyeless in Gaza* and *Crome Yellow*. The country houseparty in *Crome Yellow* is modelled on those he witnessed at Garsington, and Lady Ottoline Morrell was not flattered by her rendering in the novel. Another ungrateful visitor she must have thought. Huxley stayed there for a while in 1916 working on the farm, although his diseased eye would have kept him from the Front in any case.

Balliol College Library, 1912, as it would have appeared while Aldous Huxley was at Oxford.

CHAPTER FOUR

JOHN RUSKIN &
THE PRE-RAPHAELITES
IN OXFORD

It is ironic that John Ruskin, the great protagonist of Gothic architecture, should have spent his undergraduate years as gentleman commoner, 1837–42, in rooms in the severely classical Peckwater Quad of Christ Church. This photograph shows the Oxford buildings as nineteenth-century scholars saw them – stonework peeling and flaking from the grime of coal fires.

Ruskin's influence is felt everywhere in Oxford, from the school of the Pre-Raphaelites which so determined the art, writing and design of a generation to the triumphs of neo-Gothic architecture he inspired – the University Museum and its acolyte houses sprinkled around North Oxford.

The University Museum, designed and built together with Sir Henry Acland, the Professor of Anatomy, in 1855–60 was one project: to unite the architecture of the building with the science, learning and the collections within. The winning design was appropriately Venetian gothic (*The Stones of Venice* had been published in 1851) and was the work of Benjamin Woodward, who worked for a Dublin firm. The decorative stone carvings throughout the museum interior display a wonderful union of gothic art, naturalism, and Irish imagination: the O'Shea brothers were brought from Dublin to carve them. However, while Ruskin was praising 'the genius of the unassisted workman who gathered out of nature the materials he needed', the O'Sheas were running away with their subject matter, making caricatures of famous people, and had to be sent home; the work was not finished until after the turn of the century.

The University Museum is seen here from the corner of South Parks Road. The Chemistry Laboratory, with its tall chimneys at each corner, was inspired by the Abbot's Kitchen at Glastonbury.

etail of the entrance doorway, in a style unique to the museum.

Inside, the pointed arch is supreme, a monument to the hitherto unrecognised artistic potential of the 'railway materials', glass and steel.

The interior in its original splendour: every surface contributes to the decoration; every material fits its function and illustrates a scientific specimen.

Another project of Ruskin's was designed to illustrate the dignity of simple but worthwhile labour to the academic mind. In 1874 a group of undergraduates was selected for a team of workers to improve the road at North Hinksey. They were also to beautify it 'as if it were a cathedral', with flower borders. The team included Oscar Wilde, who, though physically strong, was never known to take exercise of any kind, and hated getting up in the morning.

Ruskin lived simply at a cottage nearby, now known as Ruskin's Cottage and identified by a memorial plaque.

The Crown and Thistle, Bridge Street, Abingdon, *c.* 1880. Ruskin stayed here for much of 1871 after having been made Slade Professor of Art at Oxford. He drove the 4 miles to Oxford by coach, and later took rooms in Corpus Christi College.

CHAPTER FIVE

WILLIAM MORRIS
& KELMSCOTT

When he came up to Exeter College in 1853, Morris had rooms in Hell Quad overlooking Brasenose Lane, the Fellows' Garden and the Bodleian Library. Here he met Rossetti and Burne-Jones, and Jane Burden at the theatre, relationships that were to determine the rest of his life.

This is the Broad Street frontage of Exeter College as it appeared by the time Morris left Oxford, decayed stonework and old houses where the New Bodleian is now. The range to the left of the tower, hiding the Old Ashmolean Museum building, dates from 1833, but the nearer range with distinct pointed arched windows is by Scott, 1856, as is the chapel.

The Quadrangle of Exeter, with the apse of Scott's chapel, where there is now a tapestry designed by Burne-Jones and made by Morris in 1890.

The Oxford Union Society building, otherwise known as the Students' Union, on St Michael Street, 1880s. It was newly built when Morris was at Oxford, and the roof gallery of the Debating Room was decorated by him, Rossetti, Burne-Jones and others, in lively scenes from the 'Morte d'Arthur'. Little is left of the original scheme, as the technique of wall painting was hardly accomplished and they are much decayed.

After finishing at Oxford in 1857, Morris decided on architecture as a career, and secured a place in the practice of the Gothic Revival architect G.E. Street, who had an office at 15 Beaumont Street, in the same building where the author Henry James later stayed in 1894. It was a useful experience, because he met Philip Webb there, and afterwards formed a partnership with him in the arts and crafts movement furniture and design business. G.E. Street moved his practice to London.

The romantic ruins of Godstow nunnery would have appealed to Morris and William de Morgan as they made their boat trip up the Thames from Kelmscott in Hammersmith to Kelmscott Manor near Lechlade, beyond Oxford.

In 1871 the remarkable threesome of William and Jane Morris and Dante Gabriel Rossetti moved into Kelmscott Manor, in the furthest reaches of the upper Thames valley. William loved the peace of 'Kelmscott and the river', which reminded him of the then pleasant Essex lowlands, but Rossetti was often in ill health, found the house cold and draughty, and was in love with Jane. The *ménage à trois* was probably not what it appeared to the astonished villagers, as William was often away on travels for background to his writing, to Iceland to research the sagas, and found it painful to be around the pair. In 1874 he suggested he might let Rossetti take over the lease as he was seldom there, and Rossetti, instead of using it as a weekend retreat, seemed to have taken up residence. However, it did not come to this, as Rossetti became more and more ill, to the point of paranoia, and left. The attraction between Jane and Rossetti did not diminish, and some of William's most touching poetry reflects his sadness, and Jane's, at not succeeding in love.

From *Short Poems and Sonnets*:

> Then face to face we sit, a wall of lies
> Made hard by fear and faint anxieties
> Is drawn between us and he goes away
> And leaves me wishing it were yesterday.

And from *The Earthly Paradise*:

> Sweet seemed the word she spake, while it might be
> As wordless music – But truth fell on me
> And kiss and word I knew, and, left alone,
> Face to face seemed I to a wall of stone,
> While at my back there beat a boundless sea.

Kelmscott Manor is shown here in about 1885. The house is largely seventeenth century, enlarged around a medieval core, and William Morris enjoyed ripping out some later improvements, thus making it even more draughty and uncomfortable. It is open to the public twice a week in the summer.

The tapestry-hung bed at Kelmscott, with Morris' hangings and wallpaper.

Kelmscott village and pub. Morris was passionate about preserving the use of local materials in farm buildings, and in repairs to walls, cottages and barns. In this he sometimes found himself at odds with the local farmers, who had utility, not the view, or art and craft, in mind. In Kelmscott in the 1870s hardly a foreign brick or slate was to be found, and later Morris often wrote to complain when he saw cheaper replacements creeping in. The founding of the Society for the Protection of Ancient Buildings (SPAB) was the result of his anger at seeing unsympathetic renovations in the local churches, particularly of the Cotswolds, Burford and Tewkesbury. He single-handedly saved Inglesham from the hands of the Victorian restorer, Sir Gilbert Scott.

One of the attractions of Kelmscott was the window on to the life of ordinary country people, their work, handicraft, and diversions. This village 'one-man band' was photographed by Henry Taunt in about 1900.

The thirteenth-century Tithe Barn at Great Coxwell fits well with the pre-Raphaelites' view of architecture: it was Gothic, simple, useful, and above all unmodernised and unrestored. (The door in the gable end is in fact a later insertion.) William Morris revered it: 'Unapproachable in its dignity, as beautiful as a cathedral, yet with no ostentation of the builder's art.'

A scene of haymaking was recounted in *News from Nowhere*, in the countryside of the socialist utopian future, where honest labour is valued and machines do not replace men (or women) – perhaps inspired by scenes such as this near Kelmscott at the turn of the century. But did Morris really understand what backbreaking, ageing work haymaking, harvesting by hand, threshing and winnowing had been for country people?

Morris was given a simple countryman's funeral and his body was brought to Kelmscott on a flower-covered wagon for burial in the churchyard. He had been suffering from gout and other problems for a few years, but his doctor said he died from having done the work of ten men in his life. Philip Webb, who had designed William and Jane's first house in Bexleyheath, used the idea of a long, barn-like roof in his tombstone. Jane is also buried there; their daughters Jenny and May continued to live at Kelmscott.

CHAPTER SIX

OXFORD AS WONDERLAND:
CHARLES DODGSON/LEWIS CARROLL

Lewis Carroll, the real life mathematics don at Christ Church, Charles Dodgson, entertained the three young daughters of Dean Henry Liddell, one of whom was Alice, with fantasy tales woven around the rivers, meadows trees, and wildlife around them, and laced them with satire and spoof on life in the University. This is Christ Church Cathedral and one of the many gardens.

Alice's Garden – the private garden of her father the Dean.

The chestnut tree in the Deanery garden.

It began with a rowing excursion in a boat in 1862, upriver to Godstow, as a treat for Alice and her sisters. They pass Binsey, where the well of St Frideswide, known as the 'treacle well' for its healing properties, is transformed into the home of three sisters who lived on treacle at the bottom of the well. The story unfolds as they wind upriver, taking in the rabbit holes and other river life, with allusions to the college landmarks familiar to them – curious creatures in gargoyles, the gardens and tree-lined walks. Characters of everyday acquaintance become caricatures – the Gryphon, the Mock Turtle, the bat, the drawing master, the Mad Hatter. Even the tall Alice with her ever so long neck is modelled on the fireplace furniture in the Hall of Christ Church.

These are the ruins of Godstow Nunnery from the river, a gentle curving reach lined with rushes, trees, meadows, livestock and the small animals that take on human characteristics in *Alice in Wonderland*.

Behind this lies the journey through college life – undergraduate dinners are like the Mad Hatter's tea party; a game of croquet has nightmarish rules; there are inquisitions, examinations, logic lessons, decrees, secret gardens; strange rules exclude outsiders. An allegory using the Royal visit to Oxford in 1863, which fascinated the children, embellished the story when it was finally written down and published in 1865.

This is one of Lewis Carroll's rooms in Christ Church. They were in Tom Quad, overlooking the Deanery Garden.

The Great Quad, or Tom Quad, where Dodgson had his rooms in the far corner. It is the largest in Oxford. The gothic revival hall towers over the right side.

Christ Church Hall – the largest pre-Victorian hall in either Oxford or Cambridge, according to Pevsner. Because of its grandness, it is known with typical understatement as The House.

Alice's Shop on St Aldates, opposite Christ Church, where the Liddell sisters were accustomed to buying sweets. They would not be allowed to cross the street there today.

CHAPTER SEVEN

OXFORD AS ATHENS:
OSCAR WILDE

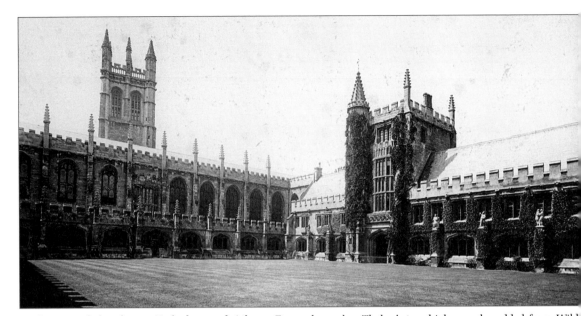

Dryden coined the phrase: 'Oxford seemed Athens, Everywhere else, Thebes', to which may be added from Wild 'For Irishmen, Oxford is to the mind what Paris is to the body.' Oscar Wilde, with the incredible initials O.F.O'F.W.W for Oscar Fingal O'Flahertie Wills Wilde, arrived in Oxford in 1874, to read 'Greats', Classics, at Magdalen, an scratched the initials on the window pane of his rooms. He was in No. 8 ground in Cloisters Quad at first, but in h fourth year he had a grander set in the Kitchen staircase, now part of the students' bar and lounge area.

Although an outstanding scholar, eventually getting a First, Wilde cultivated the art of appearing casual abou work, turning out elegantly, even foppish, in dress, and being fastidious about the décor of his rooms. He was i trouble over the work more than once, but finished brilliantly. He was sent down in 1877 for one term for n appearing back in First Week after a holiday in Greece, as he put it characteristically, 'for being the fir undergraduate to visit Olympia'. It was said he joined the Masons so as to acquire the costume; and he ran in debt furnishing his rooms. 'I find it harder and harder every day to live up to my blue china' he was widely quote as saying, and found himself referred to in the University sermon, even satirised in *Punch*. He kept lilies in h rooms because they were described as being both beautiful and useless in Ruskin's *Stones of Venice*, and boug glassware, and the famous blue china, from Spiers on the High Street, running up large debts.

Headington Hill Hall: at the May Day ball given by the Morrells, Wilde wore a startling Prince Rupe costume of plum coloured velvet and silk stockings.

A typical undergraduate's room of the 1880s. For Wilde's rooms, imagine blue china vases, cupboards full of glasses and vases of lilies.

Spiers and Son's establishment.

The Mitre, High Street, where Wilde normally took breakfast.

CHAPTER EIGHT

FROM WESSEX TO CHRISTMINSTER:
THOMAS HARDY &
JUDE THE OBSCURE

Thomas Hardy veered into northern Wessex for the setting of his tragic novel *Jude the Obscure*, to the downla
villages of Fawley, Letcombe Bassett, and Wantage town: Marygreen, Cresscombe and Alfredston in the book. Th
relic landscape which displays marvels of prehistory at every turn, and is full of romantic vistas, popular picn
spots, and circular walks and rides has a sinister role in Jude. Its nature is limiting – limiting in the produce of t
land and limiting to its natives – as well as threatening and menacing. For Jude, it was a 'solid barrier of c
cretaceous upland', with a 'sad, wet season'; the village green a 'patch of clammy greensward'.

There are cold spots up and down Wessex in autumn and winter weather; but the coldest of all when a nor
or east wind is blowing is the crest of the down by the Brown House, where the road to Alfredston crosses t
old Ridgeway. Here the first winter sleets and snows fall and lie, and here the spring frost lingers last unthaw
Here in the teeth of the north-east wind and rain Jude now pursued his way, wet through, the necessa
slowness of his walk from lack of his former strength being insufficient to maintain his heat. He came to t
milestone, and, raining as it was, spread his blanket and lay down there to rest.

The little brook meanders to Wantage, the market town of Alfredston, which still has peaceful corners like t
– photographed by Tom Reveley.

In contrast, Christminster, or Oxford, was the image of 'the new Jerusalem'. Jude 'could hardly believe that it rained so drearily there'. He first saw Christminster as a boy from a ladder to the top of the Brown House on the crest of the downs:

Some way within the limits of the stretch of landscape, points of light like the topaz gleamed. The air increased in transparency with the lapse of minutes, till the topaz points showed themselves to be the vanes, windows, wet roof slates, and other shining spots upon the spires, domes, free-stonework, and varied outlines that were faintly revealed. It was Christminster, unquestionably, either directly seen, or miraged in the peculiar atmosphere.

For a poor countryman to get around, miles had to be walked: Jude walked to Alfredston from Marygreen daily to learn his stonemason's craft, until he took spartan rooms there, leaving precious little time and energy for his studies. A few hours' diversion with Arabella on a Sunday afternoon kept him from his grammars for the week.

Arabella's cottage, in Jude's eye, was hardly picturesque: 'unhealthy fir trees' lined the way. 'Here at the base of the chalk formation he neared the brook that oozed from it, and followed the stream till he reached her dwelling. A smell of piggeries came from the back, and the grunting of the originators of that smell.' The first courting call was full of bad omens.

'Arabella's Cottage' along the Letcombe Brook, in Letcombe Bassett, was photographed by the Wantage photographer Tom Reveley.

And later Jude went to Christminster, to follow the dream to work his way to study for a degree:

> He now paused at the top of a crooked and gentle declivity, and obtained his first near view of the city. Grey stoned and dun-roofed it stood within hail of the Wessex border, and almost with the tip of one small toe within it, at the northernmost point of the crinkled line along which the leisurely Thames strokes the fields of that ancient kingdom. The buildings now lay quiet in the sunset, a vane here and there on their many spires and domes, giving sparkle to a picture of sober secondary and tertiary hues.

In reality it is not possible to see Oxford from the crest of the downs above Wantage, but the view of the city from Hinksey Hill may have been Jude's first close-up view, and is justly famous.

When Jude returned to Marygreen from Christminster to find Sue, the journey there and back was excruciatingly exhausting. 'It was dark when he reached Alfredston, where he had a cup of tea, the deadly chill that began to creep into his bones being too much for him to endure fasting. To get home he had to travel by a steam tramcar and two branches of a railway, with much waiting at a junction. He did not reach Christminster till ten o'clock.'

This description refers to the problematic rail connections from Oxford when the Great Western Railway line was first built: the main line from London to Swindon went through Didcot because of opposition from the University. When a branch line was finally built, many journeys from Oxford had to be broken with a wait at Didcot junction. From Didcot, Jude would have taken the Great Western train to Wantage Road station, which was located 2 miles north of the town. The Wantage Tramway connected the station to the town terminus on Mill Street. From there Jude would have had a 5-mile walk to Marygreen, or Fawley, over the crest of the downs. To make a return journey on the same day was arduous.

The Matthews No. 6 engine is standing at Wantage Road station. The Tramway Company bought this engine in 1888; it was in passenger service until 1925, and Jude might well have travelled on it!

At Christminster, Jude never crossed the boundary between town and gown; he remained an outsider. He lodged in the narrow lanes with mean houses squeezed in between the great college grounds. The Encaenia procession of Remembrance Day in the book, watched in a crowd from Radcliffe Square, symbolised everything that was part of the dream, and his exclusion from it. This one is from 1899, passing in front of Hertford College.

Christ Church, the 'Cardinal College' of Jude's dreams, presents a cloister wall to St Aldates, incorporating a bastion of the medieval city wall. 'and all down there is Cardinal with its long front, and its windows with lifted eyebrows, representing the polite surprise of the University at the efforts of such as I' reflects Jude, as he says goodbye to his dream.

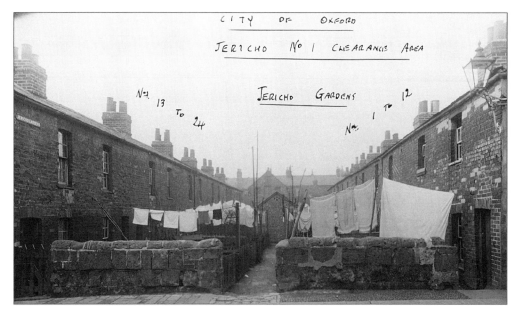

On his return to Christminster, at the low point of their fortunes, Jude found lodgings for himself, Sue and the three children in the poor area of Beersheba, or Jericho, around the University Press and the Oxford Canal. These houses are in the 'brick skirt' surrounding the town centre which so appalled Gerard Manley Hopkins and were recalled in his poem *Duns Scotus's Oxford*. The nearby church of St Barnabas, St Silas in the novel, was built in 1869 at the expense of the Superintendent of the Press, in a severe, undecorated, neo-Romanesque style, and appears as gloomy as the rest of the area – a suitable stage for the sad scene enacted there.

Arabella, however, found enough diversion in the life of the publicans, tradesmen and fringes of college life. Her father ran a 'miserable little pork and sausage shop' and they were of 'a certain class at Christminster who knew not the colleges, nor their works, nor their ways'. When Jude lay dying, she couldn't help being drawn through the gardens of Cardinal College, at the invitation of some of the workmen, to the river to see the rowing and bumps of the Eights Week races, when college barges lined the river and townspeople promenaded along the towpath. This one dates from the 1890s.

CHAPTER NINE

THOMAS HUGHES:
TOM BROWN'S SCHOOLDAYS &
TOM BROWN AT OXFORD

Uffington, Thomas Hughes' birthplace in 1822, inspired and formed the setting for his best-known works, *To Brown's Schooldays* (1857), *The Scouring of the White Horse* (1859) and *Tom Brown at Oxford*. The features of the landscape of the White Horse were full of myth and mystery for Hughes as a child: the prehistoric burial chamber of Wayland's Smithy, the Blowing Stone, the numerous relic sarsen stones, or 'grey wethers', of the downs, and the White Horse itself. As a man, he rued the changes in the farming practices on the downs, which were turning the wild scenery of legend, open pasture and scrubland into a tame sward of heavily manured fodder and cereal crops.

Grandson of the vicar, Hughes attended the little chalk school, now a museum named after Tom Brown, and went on to prep school in Hampshire, Rugby, and Oriel College, Oxford. His return to the village for the scouring of the White Horse, the seven-yearly fête of games, contests, shows, and picnics which accompanied the ritual trimming of the turf from the chalk outline of the horse on Uffington Hill, is recounted in the book. Description is attended with much philosophising by old village characters:

God meant these downs, Sir, for sheep-walks, and so our fathers left them; but within the last twenty years would-be wise men have found that they will grow decent turnips and not very bad oats. Well, they plough them up, and find two inches of soil only, get one crop cut of them, and spoil them for sheep. Next year, more crops. Then comes manure, manure, manure – nothing but expense; not a turnip will trouble itself to grow bigger than a radish under a pennyworth of guano or bones. The wise men grumble and swear, but the downs are spoiled. . . . They are all mad for ploughing, Sir, these blockhead farmers; why, half of them keep their sheep standing on boards all the year round. They would plough and grow mangold-wurzel on their fathers graves. The Tenth Legion, Sir, has probably marched along this road. . . .

This is the White Horse, possibly enhanced by the photographer, from Uffington.

Tom Brown's School, as it would have appeared in Hughes' time, photographed in the 1880s by Henry Taunt.

Industrious schoolboys of a later age working the allotment gardens at Uffington in 1916, with the thirteenth-century lantern tower of the church in which Hughes was baptised and the downs beyond.

The White Horse, of debatable date from Iron Age to Saxon, but revered for long enough to be beyond even fol memory. Thomas Hughes recorded all the known 'scourings' from sources over a hundred years before he wa born.

A fête, similar to that described by Hughes in his book, on Uffington Castle, the hill fort above the White Horse.

All along the north side were the theatres and peep-shows, and acrobats, and the pink-eyed lady, and the other shows. On the west side were the publicans' booths . . . and the great street of hucksters' stalls and cheap Jacks was all set out along the south side . . . the gipsies and people with no regular businesses were all got away into a corner, behind the stalls. . . . About the middle of the camp stood a large stage about six feet high, roped round for the backswording and wrestling.

A boy is about to get a slide down the ramparts!

Tom Brown at Oxford takes the country boy up to Oxford to discover the life of the undergraduate – falling in love and out of love; hunting, drinking and getting close to trouble; having exploits; running up debts; and finally developing character – but little mention of studies. This image of college life has a long history which even now has not completely been dispelled.

This illustration is from the 1897 edition of the book: an undergraduate 'breakfast'.

CHAPTER TEN

THE GARSINGTON SET
& THEIR VISITORS

At Garsington, on a beautiful ridge overlooking Oxford, many literary and artistic figures, and not only those to be found at the University, visited the home of Lady Ottoline Morrell. She fell in love with the small Elizabethan manor house when she toured the neighbourhood with her husband Philip after their marriage. They lived there from 1915 to 1928. Philip, an MP, was a pacifist during the First World War, and they harboured a number of conscientious objectors, even seeing that agricultural war work was provided to enable them to avoid conscription.

The village is centred around the cross and war memorial.

Village life was far removed from life in the Manor, but Ottoline allowed the village schoolchildren to use the pool for swimming lessons, built a new village hall, and set up a library in the manor.

Ottoline planned from the outset to make her home a magnet for the literary and artistic crowd of that generation. Her somewhat uncommunicative husband did not restrain her, even though the couple were not nearly as wealthy as the appearance they gave. A phaeton carriage would collect the weekend's visitors from Wheatley station. Ottoline had decorated the house in sea green, Venetian red and a good deal of gold beading around the panelled rooms, and distributed Persian carpets and blue and white china everywhere. With real flair, she created the Italianate garden and swimming pool, still one of the attractions of the region on the garden open days.

The front of Garsington manor.

The seventeenth-century south front, with the garden sloping down towards the fishponds, is seen here in 1913.

The south front of Garsington Manor. Regular visitors were Lytton Strachey, who came for weeks at a time, and Dora Carrington, Katherine Mansfield, Bertrand Russell (with whom Ottoline had a long affair), Duncan Grant, Vanessa and Clive Bell, and Virginia Woolf – a roll call of the Bloomsbury set.

Aldous Huxley was introduced to the group as a young student at Balliol, and brought his young friends there. He described a comical night spent sleeping on the roof, with the noise of owls, geese and peacocks, and the romantic setting of the garden at a Garsington house-party in *Crome Yellow*:

> That part of the garden that sloped down from the foot of the terrace to the pool had a beauty which did not depend on colour so much as on forms. It was as beautiful by moonlight as in the sun. The silver of water, the dark shapes of yew and ilex trees remained, at all hours and seasons, the dominant features of the scene. It was a landscape in black and white. For colour there was the flower-garden; it lay to one side of the pool, separated from it by a huge Babylonian wall of yews. You passed through a tunnel in the hedge, you opened a wicket in a wall, and you found yourself, startlingly and suddenly, in the world of colour.

A special friend and visitor was D.H. Lawrence, who built the summer house, raved over the garden with Ottoline and was glad of the refuge and the hospitality. He left the manuscript of *The Rainbow* with Ottoline when he went to Florida during the obscenity hearings – all copies of the book had been burnt. But Freida was jealous of the friendship; there was more than one scene, and the Lawrences left for good to live in Cornwall. Ottoline was rewarded for her generosity with an unflattering reflection of herself as Hermione in *Women in Love*.

In fact, most of the Bloomsbury set who were happy to visit, eat well during the war, escape London and privations elsewhere, gossiped and wrote unkind letters about Ottoline to each other afterwards, after writing the customary fulsome thank-you notes.

CHAPTER ELEVEN

THE OXFORD OF
BRIDESHEAD REVISITED

CHRISTCHURCH, OXFORD.

For many writers, Christ Church, The House, was Oxford. Here was set probably the most famous Oxford novel of all, Evelyn Waugh's *Brideshead Revisited*. Sebastian Flyte, the aristocrat tragic character, was a student here; his ironic and less well-off friend, Charles Ryder, was at another less exalted college. It was not the First World War that changed Oxford or challenged its elitism – student life between the wars provided the opportunity for good living, hilarious parties, learning about champagne, wine and manners, and making lifelong friends and connections. It was country house living, but in grand communal surroundings provided by some of the most beautiful architecture, albeit crumbling, to be found from any period from the Middle Ages onwards.

Christ Church and St Aldates are seen here in the 1920s. The motor car was beginning its encroachment on to the peace of the University town. Undergraduates were allowed to keep cars under licence from the Proctor, and under strict rules: a car could not be kept within 20 miles of Oxford except under licence; a car could not be kept in the first three terms; the car had to be kept at a named garage and could only be used between 1 (except at weekends) and 11pm; written consents from the proctor or the Dean of the college had to be obtained for any variation to the rules. These rules were still in force well into the 1950s, when an undergraduate had to display a green lamp on the car to identify it. Still, the car afforded the opportunity to travel outside the city boundaries – to fashionable inns such as The Spread Eagle, Thame, for example. Anthony Blanche borrows a car to take Charles Ryder to dinner to talk about Sebastian and the Flyte family: 'There is a delightful hotel there, which luckily doesn't appeal to the Bullingdon.' (The Bullingdon Club was for wealthy, hearty, loud undergraduates.)

Anthony Blanche eulogised the college's beauty at sunset, before being taken by a crowd of undergraduates out into Tom Quad and ducked in the fountain under the statue of Mercury: 'We put him in Mercury' as they would brag in later life. The statue is a copy of a Mercury by Giovanni da Bologna, and was given to the college in 1928. The pedestal is by Lutyens.

Within the college walls, such as this imposing corner of Peckwater Quad and the Library of Christ Church, one is transported into another world of privilege, of insider knowledge as to how to behave, speak and dress, of nothing unpleasant to the eye.

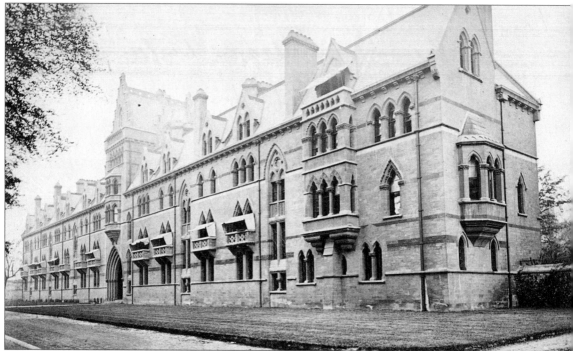

Sebastian Flyte had rooms in the Meadow Buildings: from his balcony after a lavish lunch, Anthony Blanche shouted down lines from 'The Waste Land' at the students on their way to the river.

Although *Brideshead Revisited* was set in Christ Church, Waugh himself was a student at Hertford (1922–4), and observed the antics of his aristocratic contemporaries more from the Charles Ryder point of view. Like John Betjeman, he whiled away too many hours in flamboyant behaviour and found himself at odds with his tutor. He managed a bad Third-class degree, but retaliated with a string of hugely popular novels, some grown from the life and people he knew at Oxford.

THE MODERN SCENE:
AUDEN, THE INKLINGS,
DYLAN THOMAS

W.H. Auden arrived at Christ Church the year Waugh left. The aspirations of the intellectuals of the University began to be expressed in an interest in politics, serious writing and commitment rather than total immersion in aestheticism. Auden was Professor of Poetry from 1956 to 1960, and the College gave him the Brewhouse on the edge of the Meadow to live in during his final few years, 1972–4.

C. Day Lewis was one of 'The Gang' of poets and writers whom Auden gathered around him. He was at Wadham, and taught at Summer Fields on Banbury Road after his degree, in order to prolong his stay in Oxford. He lived over the gate lodge. The left-wing inclinations of 'The Gang' turned him towards Communism in the '30s, and he gave up teaching in public schools. His experiences provided ample material for a novel, and soon, under the name Nicholas Blake, he was able to support his life as a poet through writing detective stories. His term as Professor of Poetry began in 1951.

C.S. Lewis, as fellow of Magdalen from 1924 to 1954, presided over a generation of undergraduates in English literature, spanning the '20s and '30s and post-Second World War era. He wrote some of his best-known books here: *The Allegory of Love*, *The Problem of Pain*, *The Screwtape Letters* and *The Lion, the Witch and the Wardrobe*. He had rooms in the New Buildings of Magdalen, and also shared a house with his brother, also an academic, in Kiln Lane, Headington. The house has been bought by a Trust of devotees, who have been hoping to restore it and open it to the public. He is buried in the parish churchyard of Headington Quarry.

Magdalen College, Cloister Quad and the New Buildings are shown here. The Mill House where A.J.P. Taylor lived, and the summerhouse where Dylan Thomas stayed, are in the line of trees beyond.

Lines on the New Buildings, Magdalen College, Oxford (composed by the Rev. James Hurdis DD (1763–1801), sometime Professor of Poetry at Oxford. They were added to by John Betjeman in 1980:

> How gracefully it rests upon its shadow
> In the deep quiet of this walled-in meadow,
> Grave, grey and classical and on its own
> A hymn by Addison in Oxford stone
> Magdalen New Buildings! Glad was I when young
> To hear, in your wide arch, the quarters rung. . . .

C.S. Lewis, with J.R.R. Tolkien and Charles Williams, were known as The Inklings, and shared an interest in writing and talking about the legendary, the metaphysical, the religious, the mysterious, and the magic of the life unseen and the imagination. Many of these discussions took place in the Eagle and Child pub on St Giles in the 1940s and early '50s.

Several houses in Oxford are associated with Tolkien: they include 3 Manor Road (left), 20 Northmoor Road (below), 22 Northmoor Road (opposite, top), 76 Sandfield Road (opposite, middle) and 99 Holywell (opposite bottom). The gabled house, centre, is no. 100; part of 99, which has two further gables, just appears on the right of the picture.

Tolkien is buried in Wolvercote Cemetery, along with Joyce Cary (d. 1957) and Sir James Murray, editor of the *Oxford English Dictionary*, 1885.

Joyce Cary, 1888–1957, came up to Oxford in 1909 after training in art at Edinburgh and rejecting that career – he read law at Trinity, got a fourth, and went to the Balkans as a Red Cross medical orderly in 1912. He then joined the colonial service and spent the next eight years in West Africa.

Cary had met Gertrude Ogilvie, the sister of a good friend, while at Oxford, and they married in 1916. When he retired from service in Africa in 1920 (he was wounded in the Nigerian Regiment in the Cameroons) they settled at 12 Parks Road. His Irish childhood, love of art, political and colonial experiences were the inspiration of his novels, which were all written from this time until his death in 1957.

Dylan Thomas and Caitlin were more than once helped out by Margaret Taylor, wife of the historian A.J.P. Taylor, fellow of Magdalen College. The family stayed with them for Christmas in 1945 and was able to rent the summerhouse in the garden of the Mill by the Cherwell, at Holywell Ford. Thomas amused himself watching the water voles.

To Vernon Watkins, April 1946:

> Right below where we live – it is, I think, a converted telephone kiosk, with a bed where the ledge for directories used to be – there is a vole-run. . . . The run is so narrow that two voles cannot pass each other. Suddenly, an elderly, broad vole with a limp came quite fast down the run from the left just as an elderly, broader vole with a limp came from the right. From where I am sitting, expectantly nervous and ill like patient on an imminent, I could see what the voles were thinking. They never stopped running as they thought, as they neared one another. Who was to turn back? should they both turn back? should they fight, kiss, call it a day, lie down? They never stopped their limping running as I saw and heard the decision made. With a wheezing like that of a little otter, with a husky squeaky updrawing of shining arthritic legs, the elderly broader limping vole jumped over the back of the other. Not a word was said.

While in Oxford, Dylan Thomas used to drink regularly here, at the Port Mahon, at St Clements.

ter, Margaret Taylor bought The Manor House at South Leigh for the Thomases, 'small and a bit battered, but
ght in a village and in good country', only twenty-five minutes from Oxford by train. But the two years spent
ere were not successful for Thomas: his drinking was increasing and he was doing little work. He moaned about
ountry life in his letters.

Robert Pocock, April 1948:
The landlord of the Fleece has nearly lost his eye, our dog Mable has eczema, our cat Satan had mange and is
now dead, Caitlin has gone to London with Margaret Taylor & left me quite alone, the house beer has run out, I
am 3 weeks behind with my filmscript, not having started it yet, my gas fire has just exploded, I have flooded the
kitchen with boiling soup, I am broke. Caitlin has taken the cigarettes, I was suddenly sick in the middle of the
night, Phil has just sent me his 25 shilling book about Hampton Court, rabbits have eaten the lettuce, and seven
cows, who have opened the gate, are trying to get into the lavatory. There is no news. Ever, Dylan.

South Leigh station in the 1950s. What a pity all these rural stations have been closed. Soon afterwards, Margaret Taylor bought the Boat House at Laugharne, in Wales, where Thomas lived until his death.

CHAPTER THIRTEEN

JOHN BETJEMAN

John Betjeman spent both his early schooldays and his university days in Oxford, first at the Dragon School, then, after Marlborough School in Wiltshire, at Magdalen College. His autobiographical poem 'Summoned by Bells' (1960) recalls a boyhood shadowed by the First World War:

'And so we knitted shapeless gloves from string
For men in mine-sweepers, and on the map
We stuck the Allied flags along the Somme;'

But, 'the trenches and the guns
Meant less to us than bicycles and gangs
And marzipan and what there was for prep.

Take me, my Centaur bike, down Linton Road,
Gliding by newly planted almond trees
Where the young dons with wives in tussore clad
Were building in the morning of their lives
Houses for future Dragons. Rest an arm
Upon the post of the allotment path,
Then dare the slope! We choked in our own dust,
The narrowness of the footpath made our speed
Seem swift as light. May-bush and elm flashed by,
Allotment holders turning round to stare,
Potatoes in their hands. Speed-wobble! Help!'

The streets of pleasant North Oxford were explored by bicycle, and he became acquainted with the variety of churches, buildings and streetscapes which became his passion in life.

'Can words express the unexampled thrill
I first enjoyed in Norm., E.E., and Dec.?
Norm., crude and round and strong and primitive,
E.E., so lofty, pointed, fine and pure,
And Dec. the high perfection of it all,
Flowingly curvilinear, from which
The Perp. showed such a "'lamentable decline".'

Betjeman was unlucky as a student at Magdalen to draw C.S. Lewis as a tutor, for the two men were utterly different in their approach to life and tastes in art and literature. While Betjeman enthused over architecture, churches, lavish display in church ceremony and the aesthete's lifestyle, his tutor was of another milieu, in the imaginary, literary world of The Inklings. His teddy bear, Archie, which he carried around Oxford, was said to be the model for Sebastian Flyte's bear Aloysius in *Brideshead Revisited.*

> 'Balkan Sobranies in a wooden box,
> The college arms upon the lid; Tokay
> And sherry in the cupboard; . . .'

> 'For life was luncheons , luncheons all the way –
> And evenings dining with the Georgeoisie. . . .

> Moon after parties: moon on Magdalen Tower,
> And shadow on the place for climbing in . . .'

By his own admission, studies suffered; Betjeman failed to get his degree and left Oxford in 1928.

> Failed in Divinity! O, towers and spires!
> Could no one help? Was nothing to be done?'

After marriage to Penelope in 1933, the Betjemans lived in the Berkshire Downs, in what is now Oxfordshire, for many years: first at Garrards Farm in Uffington (pictured here) and from 1945 the large old rectory at Farnborough.

Finally they settled at The Mead, Wantage in 1951, where they lived for twenty-one years. 'This house is an ugly lit thing in a lovely setting of apple trees and meadows by a mill stream right in the centre of Wantage . . . rus in urbe.'

Betjeman concerned himself with writing: in addition to his volumes of poetry, he sometimes wrote over 1(letters a day, many as Secretary of the Oxford Preservation Trust – about the preservation of churches, c buildings, and street furniture. The offices were in Cornmarket in Oxford, where he commuted a few times a wee To Kenneth Clark in 1951, hoping to enlist the Royal Fine Art Society and the CPRE in the campaign: 'It's abc concrete lamp standards. As you probably know, Chippenham, Banbury, Salisbury, Abingdon, Crewkerr Watlington, Corsham & Wokingham are ruined by them. Wallingford and Marlborough are threatened.'

Penelope was a great local character, getting involved in good works, the Church (she later converted Catholicism) and enterprisingly running the tea rooms 'King Alfred's Kitchen' on Newbury Street. She broug the first espresso machine to Wantage and was rewarded with gangs of motorcyclists making a regular pit-st there on the way to the coast.

This is Newbury Street in the 1950s: King Alfred's Kitchen is the little shop gable-end on in the middle of t photograph. Not a concrete lamp standard to be seen.

The Betjemans moved from Wantage in 1972 to li in Cornwall. He wrote 'On Leaving Wantage, 197.

I like the way these old brick garden walls
Unevenly run down to the Letcombe Brook.
I like the mist of green about the elms
In earliest leaf-time. More intensely green
The duck weed undulates; a mud – grey trout
Hovers and darts away at my approach.

Priory Road is a peaceful street of red-and blue checkerboard brick houses whose walls run dow to the Letcombe Brook behind; the elms in the distance lead to the brook and King Alfred's Well and, oh dear, is that a concrete lamp standard next to the car?

CHAPTER FOURTEEN

WOMEN AT OXFORD –
WRITERS AT SOMERVILLE

Oxford, Somerville College.

Somerville College, founded in 1879, did not receive full college status until 1960. Rose Macaulay (*Potterism, The Towers of Trebizond*) was one of a group of successful writers who were at the college just before the First World War: they also included Dorothy L. Sayers (*Busman's Honeymoon, Gaudy Night*); Vera Brittain (*Testament of Youth, Testament of Friendship*); Winifred Holtby (*The Land of Green Ginger, South Riding*); Margaret Kennedy (*The Constant Nymph*); and Helen Waddell (*Peter Abelard*).

Dining in the newer women's colleges was in a different style from that at the traditional colleges. St Ann
College was The Society of Oxford Home Students when Naomi Haldane Mitchison (1897–1999) attended it
around the same time as the Somerville group. She was friends with W.H. Auden, and probably knew Aldo
Huxley as a family friend of the Haldanes. The family lived on St Margarets Road and then Linton Road. She
known for her rebel feminist writing, journalism, children's books, and her novels *The Conquered* (1923) about t
Romans in Gaul, and *The Corn King and the Spring Queen* (1931).

Dame Iris Murdoch, who died in 1999, aged seventy-nine, was connected with both of these women's colleg
she was an undergraduate at Somerville and a philosophy don at St Anne's; she was made honorary Fellow
both, as well as at St Catherine's where her husband Professor John Bayley held his post. She lived in Oxfordsh
and in Oxford most of her adult life. Her twenty-seven novels include many Booker and Whitbread Prize winne
such as *The Sea, The Sea, The Sacred and Profane Love Machine, The Sandcastle, The Book and the Brotherhood, 1
Black Prince, The Nice and the Good, A Severed Head. The Bell* was made into a television series, and she also wro
on philosophy, and on Sartre.

Naomi Mitchison in 1973, photographed by Ramsay and Muspratt
photographers. The two women had a studio at 23 Cornmarket for over
thirty years, and had many writers and academics as subjects. Helen
Muspratt has just recently left her collection to the centre for Oxfordshire
Studies.

CHAPTER FIFTEEN

UP & DOWN
THE RIVER

The Thames enters the county at Henley. Between Henley and near Reading it forms the border. Henley, Shiplake, Sonning, Reading, Mapledurham, Streatley, Goring, Wallingford, Shillingford, Ewelme. Dorchester, Long Wittenham, Clifton Hampden, Abingdon, Nuneham, Oxford, Godstow Stanton Harcourt, Kelmscott and Lechlade are the main places of interest.

The Thames, with its many working locks and attractive riverside pubs and villages, has inspired a number of writers, and many have chosen to live in Oxfordshire's upper reaches. Some have just visited, as Alexander Pope in 1713 and 1714, with the sisters Teresa and Martha Blount at Mapledurham, an Elizabethan pile near Reading. Tennyson married a local girl, Emily Sellwood, at Shiplake Church in 1850. W.B. Yeats took a cottage at Shillingford in the spring of 1921, where he wrote some of his poetry, before moving to Thame. Minchen's Cottage is on the road to Warborough; the Bridge and Hotel are well known.

thers, like Jerome K. Jerome, and William Morris, felt a passion for undertaking the entire journey by boat from ondon upriver – to arrive at Oxford by a picturesque route that even John Betjeman might have thought a fitting pproach.

Jerome K. Jerome made the navigation of the river famous in his comic *Three Men in a Boat*, published in 1889. hree friends, George, Harris and Jerome, the narrator, with little naval experience, rent a dubious skulling skiff, omplete with mattress and cover, at Kingston for a trip upriver as a two-week holiday. They quarrel, have nishaps, enjoy the scenery and churches, meet other sailors, lock keepers, publicans and country types, and try) wash their clothes in the river.

When Harris or George makes an ass of himself on dry land, I smile indulgently; when they behave in a chuckle-headed way on the river, I use the most blood-curdling language to them. When another boat gets in my way, I feel I want to take an oar and kill all the people in it.

Jerome is not tentative about his opinions on the places they pass either: 'one does not linger in the eighbourhood of Reading'. They like Sonning and Shiplake; they find Henley getting ready for the regatta, but niserably rainy and all the hotels full. Dorchester is 'a delightfully peaceful old place, nestling in stillness and ilence and drowsiness'; Abingdon is 'a typical country town of the smaller order – quiet, eminently respectable, lean, and desperately dull'.

The Thames at Shiplake. Punch lampooned Jerome as 'Arry K. Arry', after the description of an encounter with a boat party of provincial 'Arries and 'Arriets, but the book was an enormous success.

Wittenham Clumps, two outlying hills from the nearby downs, photographed from the river near Days Lock, by Henry Taunt – a scene you can still find.

The party came across the Barley Mow at Clifton Hampden (seen here in 1877), of which the men approved: 'a wonderfully pretty village, old-fashioned, peaceful and dainty with flowers, the river scenery is rich and beautiful. If you stay the night on land at Clifton, you cannot do better than put up at the Barley Mow. It is, without exception, I should say, the quaintest, most old world inn up the river. It stands on the right of the bridge, quite away from the village. Its low-pitched gables and thatched roof and latticed windows give it quite a story-book appearance, while inside it is even still more once-upon-a-timeyfied.'

By 1910 the Barley Mow was painted in the black-and-white style it sports today, and had a cottage extension built on the back. The quaint thatched roof has suffered more than one fire. 'It would not be a good place for the heroine of a modern novel to stay at. The heroine of a modern novel is always "divinely tall", and she is ever "drawing herself up to her full height". At the Barley Mow she would bump her head against the ceiling each time she did this.'

Clifton Lock in 1884, and a pretty stretch of towpath and river bank. 'We were up early the next morning, as we wanted to be in Oxford by the afternoon. It is surprising how early one can get up, when camping out. One does not yearn for "just another five minutes" nearly so much, lying wrapped up in a rug on the boards of a boat, with a Gladstone bag for a pillow, as one does in a feather bed. We had finished breakfast, and were through Clifton lock by half past eight.' They obviously did not take their own advice and stay at the Barley Mow!

Jerome is buried in Ewelme churchyard, seen here from a distance; there are three family tombs by the path leading to the rectory. Geoffrey Chaucer visited his granddaughter Alice in Ewelme. The fine tombs of Thomas Chaucer, his son, and Alice de la Pole, who married the Duke of Suffolk, and endowed the almshouses and free school, are inside the church. There is also a handy family tree showing the Chaucer relationship with John of Gaunt's line.

A view of Clifton Bridge in 1887 – the bridge is of red brick, and dates from the Victorian rebuilding of 1864 by G.G. Scott.

The Poet Laureate John Masefield lived nearby at Burcote Brook from 1939 until his death in 1967. The house has since burned down. He loved the countryside of Oxfordshire, having once kept the farmhouse at Lollingdon Down, but in 1963 he wrote of Oxford in a letter: 'I saw Oxford as a quiet little grey city beginning to have a noisome red rash all round it. I have not been to it for over 10 years.' What would he think now?

The downland scenery is apt to prompt musing on the natural world. The huge skies swept with whatever the weather brings are a constant reminder of the fragility of man's place in the landscape. The signs of past human activity, the Ridgeway, the Roman roads, quarries, hillforts, barrows and burial mounds put the present in its place. In 1917 John Masefield wrote from Lollingdon Downs, near Wallingford:

> I could not sleep for thinking of the sky,
> The unending sky, with all its million suns
> Which turn their planets ever-lastingly
> In nothing, where the fine-haired comet runs.

This is the Saxon royal barrow on Lowbury Hill, Blewbury Down.

Sweet Thames Run Softly (1940) and *Till I End My Song* (1957) are linked to the Thames at Long Wittenham, where the author Robert Gibbings wrote and illustrated the books with his own woodcuts. He lived at Footbridge Cottage in this village at the foot of Wittenham Clumps, on the river and a stone's throw from Clifton Hampden. He died in 1958 and is buried in the churchyard.

Footbridge Cottage is opposite the cross, one of many tiled and thatched cottages in this pretty village with its long street.

A lane lined with farmhouse and barns, leading to the church.

The three men in a boat passed Nuneham Courtenay and Nuneham Park. The house contained 'a fine collection of pictures and curiosities', which could be then visited. Oliver Goldsmith took a different view in 1770. On seeing the grounds of Nuneham Courtenay and the new estate village by the turnpike road, he wrote the poem 'The Deserted Village'. The deserted medieval village stands for an honest bygone age of sturdy smiths, dusky brows, village swains and maids, and the magnificent mansion was a display of unnecessary opulence, even theft, from the poor labourers. The poem was controversial. To some the incipient romanticism and overstatement did no service to the serious issue of the impoverishment of many rural communities during the Enclosures of the eighteenth and early nineteenth centuries, the depopulation of the countryside, and the reliance of farm labourers on wages rather than land – issues about which Goldsmith felt strongly.

> The shelter'd cot, the cultivated farm
> The never failing brook, the busy mill
> The decent church that topp'd the neighbouring hill
> The hawthorn bush, with seats beneath the shade,
> For talking age and whisp'ring lovers made. . . ,
>
> A time there was, ere England's griefs began
> When every rood of ground maintain'd its man. . . .
>
> Sweet smiling village, loveliest of the lawn,
> Thy sport are fled, and all thy charms withdrawn
> Amidst thy bowers the tyrant's hand is seen,
> And desolation saddens all thy green. . . .
>
> The man of wealth and pride
> Takes up a space that many poor supplied
> Space for his lake, his park's extended bounds
> Space for his horses, equipage, and hounds
> The robe that wraps his limbs in silken sloth
> Has robb'd the neighbouring fields of half their growth.

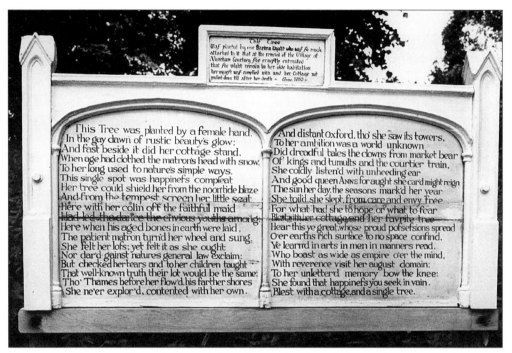

The following is the inscription shown on the memorial tablet:

This Tree
was planted by one Barbara Wyatt who was so much
attached to it that at the removal of the Village of
Nuneham Courtenay she earnestly entreated
that she might remain in her olde habitation
her wough was complied with and her Cottage not
pulled down till after her death   Anno 1780

This Tree was planted by a female hand.
In the gay dawn of rustic beauty's glow;
And fast beside it did her cottage stand,
When age had clothed the matron's head with snow.
To her long used to nature's simple ways,
This single spot was happiness compleat
Her tree could shield her from the noontide blaze
And from the tempest screen her little seat.
Here with her colin oft the faithful maid
Had led the dance the envious youths among;
Here when his aged bones in earth were laid,
The patient matron turn'd her wheel and sung.
She felt her loss; yet felt it as she ought
Nor dar'd gainst natures general law exclaim;
But checked her tears and to her children taught
That well-known truth their lot would be the same:
Tho' Thames before her flow'd his farther shores
She ne'er explor'd, contented with her own.

And distant Oxford, tho' she saw its towers,
To her ambition was a world unknown
Did dreadful tales the clowns from market bear
Of kings and tumults and the courtier train.
She coldly listen'd with unheeding ear
And good queen ANNE for aught she card might reign
The sun her day, the seasons mark'd her year
She toild, she slept, from care and envy free
For what had she to hope, or what to fear
Blest with her cottage, and her favrite tree
Hear this ye great, whose proud possessions spread
O'er earths rich surface to no space confin'd.
Who boast as wide as empire o'er the mind,
With reverence visit her august domain:
To her unletter'd memory bow the knee:
She found that happiness you seek in vain,
Blest with a cottage, and a single tree.

Inscription to Barbara Wyatt, the last of the village, who planted the tree known as Bab's Tree –
and was allowed to stay in her old cottage after the village was replaced by the new estate houses.

The view from the terrace of Nuneham Courtenay, which overlooks the estate and stretches to the
banks of the river. Home of the Earl of Harcourt, the house was partly built of stones brought from
Stanton Harcourt, the family seat on the other side of the county, and from Cogges Manor Farm,
near Witney. Cogges, another long-deserted medieval village, was also part of their estate, and the
large manor house, downgraded to a tenant farm, was falling into disrepair.

The landscaped parkland, which replaced the open fields and village.

The new estate village straddles either side of the Oxford to Dorchester road, which saw nothing noisier than a coach and horses in the 1770s, and probably was a great improvement on the medieval village cottages.

'Iffley lock and mill, a mile before you reach Oxford, is a favourite subject with the river-loving brethren of the brush. The real article, however, is rather disappointing, after the pictures. Few things I have noticed, come quite up to the pictures of them, in this world.' (Jerome K. Jerome)

This is Iffley Mill and weir at the Lock in 1888, the much-painted scene: judge for yourself. There was a catastrophic fire in 1908.

Between Iffley and Oxford is the most difficult bit of the river I know. You want to be born on that bit of water to understand it. I have been over it a fairish number of times, but I have never been able to get the hang of it. The man who could row a straight course from Oxford to Iffley ought to be able to live comfortably, under one roof, with his wife, his mother-in-law, his eldest sister, and the old servant who was in the family when he was a baby.

First the current drives you on to the right bank, and then on to the left, then it takes you out into the middle, turns you round three times, and carries you up-stream again, and always ends by trying to smash you up against a college barge.

Of course as a consequence of this, we got in the way of a good many other boats, during the mile, and they in ours, and, of course, as a consequence of that, a good deal of bad language occurred.

Jerome K. Jerome might have seen a scene like this, of watercress harvesting at Ewelme, after he came to live at Gould's Grove on the hill. He died here in 1927.

CHAPTER SIXTEEN

AROUND OXFORD

John Fothergill (1876–1957) was a gentleman, of an old Lakeland family, and educated at St John's College, Oxford. He knew the literary set of the time, which included Wilde, Shaw, Wells, Waugh, the Sitwells and Chesterton, as well as actors and painters. He was more a connoisseur and dilettante than writer himself, but his book *An Innkeeper's Diary*, published in 1931 was a once-only gem and a sell-out for its wit and gossipy style.

He started a second marriage at the age of forty-six and sought what he thought might be an undemanding life as innkeeper of a market town hotel near Oxford – the Spread Eagle in Thame – at the time 'very shabby but very possible'. 'The Inn was always empty save on Tuesdays, when a hundred farmers and kindred trades over ran the place, literally from top to bottom – we were not in it but the dirt and noise was. We were frightened to death.'

'I saw my chance of running a most splendid farmers' pandaemonium in this almost unknown patch of rural England.'

It was to become pandaemonium indeed, a small market town's Fawlty Towers, but did not remain unknown for long. The farmers, freemasons, commercial travellers and charabanc parties were soon replaced by a different type of trade altogether. Fothergill had an extensive network of rich and famous friends, and Thame was within reach of wealthy undergraduates with their new motor cars. The Bloomsbury set visited often: Fothergill was an excellent cook and kept a serious cellar. He also took it on himself to teach the undergraduates good manners, and pass comment on their choice and treatment of young ladies when necessary. 'I proposed to the Proctors that in my own interest they might "approve" us as they do the city restaurants, and though they said it was the first time they had ever thought of outside places, it was done there & then.'

Dora Carrington, artist and friend of Lytton Strachey, painted a design for a new standing signpost of the inn to replace one made a hundred years earlier, in 1824, by the local smith. This hung by brackets from the wall and was threatening to bring down the façade. After some negotiations with the local planning officers, Fothergill was granted permission to place the signpost on the pavement, at his own expense. This 1930s photograph dates from just after Fothergill sold the Spread Eagle: his name is no longer below the Spread Eagle on the sign. But 'Lunch is now Ready'.

A blue plaque now commemorates John Fothergill's inn-keeping days there, from 1922 to 1932.

The Old Grammar School, Thame, near the church, founded in the sixteenth century in a benefaction of Lord Williams, an official in the court of Henry VII. The local hero of the Civil War, John Hampden (d. 1643), went to school here, as did Dr John Fell, Dean of Christ Church, Bishop of Oxford and originator of the Fell type (1625–86), and the antiquary historian Anthony Wood (1632–95). The school moved to more comfortable quarters on the Oxford Road in the nineteenth century.

Faringdon House has had literary associations since it was built by the poet George Pye in 1770, later Poet Laureate. He has been more praised for his elegant house than his uninspired poetry, although a family tale that the grounds were haunted, by a headless ghost of a midshipman ancestor murdered to secure the inheritance, did inspire Richard Barham's story *The Legend of Hamilton Tighe*.

In 1931 Gerald Tyrwhitt, Lord Berners (1883–1950) who had inherited the estate from a childless uncle, decided to live at Faringdon House, where his mother had been living since 1910, and was buried. Novelist, composer, painter, and wildly eccentric, he had already had a varied diplomatic career, with posts in Constantinople, Rome, and Vienna. He had definite ideas about style. Pigeons dyed pastel colours floated around the grounds, which had breathtaking views over the Thames valley and the Vale of the White Horse. House parties entertained the Bloomsbury set, and even during the war luxuries could be culled from the gardens and grounds. The Mitford sisters, who lived at Swinbrook near Burford, were frequent guests, along with Gertrude Stein, the Dalis, Huxley, Siegfried Sassoon and the Mosleys. He lunched at Garsington. The Betjemans, who had moved to nearby Uffington at about the same time, were close friends. Penelope brought her Arab horse Moti, who otherwise was a common sight in Uffington pulling a small carriage, into the drawing room to pose for paintings and photographs.

It was Berners who had the Folly built, the last great folly in England. It began as a whim, as a 'neighbour-tease' of which he was fond, and was carried out doggedly against the inevitable local opposition as a matter of principle. He won. The tower was to be limited in height to no higher than 3 ft taller than the tallest tree on the mound, and carried a notice which said: 'Members of the Public committing suicide from this tower do so at their own risk.' The octagonal gothic lantern atop a classical square column was the result of Berners, who preferred the gothic, not keeping an eye on the architect, a classicist, and the building works until the upper stages of the building were reached. The Folly was opened with a huge party in 1935. It is open to the public on occasional Sundays.

The house became a hospital during the Second World War, and after his death in 1950 it was left to Heber Percy, Berners' companion and friend, who carried on the entertainment of artists, musicians and writers.

Flora Thompson's book *Lark Rise to Candleford*, describing the hamlet childhood of a young girl in north Oxfordshire in the 1880s, was written in 1945, long after she left her birthplace at Juniper Hill. She was born in 1876 and lived in this modest cottage, End House. Her father was a stonemason and her mother struggled to raise, feed and clothe her surviving four children – ten were born altogether. The charm of the book lies in its close observation of hamlet life, seemingly from a child's point of view, but really a mine of social history about the lives of poor agricultural labourers. It was the beginning of the agricultural depression and better times could be remembered, but the story is told without self-pity.

It had always been the parents' intention to leave. When he met and married his wife the father was a stranger in the neighbourhood, working for a few months on the restoration of the church in a neighbouring parish and the end house had been taken as a temporary home. Then the children had come and other things had happened to delay the removal. They could not give notice until Michaelmas Day, or another baby was coming, or they must wait until the pig was killed or the allotment crops were brought in; there was always some obstacle, and at the end of seven years they were still at the end house and still talking almost daily about leaving it. Fifty years later the father had died there and the mother was living there alone.

Flora Thompson, *c.* 1898, around the time of her marriage.

Juniper Hill village, 'Lark Rise', with the Fox Inn, centre of this small universe – called the Waggon and Horses in the book.

The Victorian school, now a private house in Cottisford, 'Fordlow' of the book, where Laura and her brother went to school.

The forge and post office at Fringford in the 1880s. Escape from a future of marriage to a farm labourer and a grindingly hard life such as her mother had was nearly impossible, but Laura' mother was determined that her daughter should have a better future. At fourteen she was sent to the neighbouring village, Fringford, 'Candleford', to work a assistant to the postmistress, whc also ran the forge. Leaving Junipe Hill was an event; her father borrowed a horse and cart, and everyone in the hamlet watched.

'So she thought of her new trunk. This contained – as well as her everyday clothes and her personal treasures, including her collection of pressed flowers, a lock of her baby brother's fair hair, and a penny exercise book, presented by her brother Edmund and inscribed by him "Laura's Journal", in which she had promised to write every night – what her mother had spoken of as "three of everything", all made of stout white calico and trimmed with crochet edging. . . .

'Her father had made and polished the trunk and studded it with her initials in bright, brass-headed nails, and deep down in one corner of it, wrapped in tissue paper, was the new half-crown he had given her.

'The contents of the trunk, the clothes she was wearing, youth and health, and a meagre education, plus a curious assortment of scraps of knowledge she had picked up in the course of her reading, were her only assets. In fitting her out, her parents had done all they could for her. They had four younger children now to be provided for. Her future must depend upon herself and what opportunities might offer.'

eckley, a tiny village on the edge of Otmoor, is the image of rustic simplicity in R.D. Blackmore's 1876 story 'Cripps the Carrier'. Cripps lives in a cottage on the road leading out to Otmoor, fringed by its seven towns, forbidding and foreign to non-villagers. He carries parcels, people and news between the village and Oxford, and is the central figure in this elaborate story of intrigue, interplay between town and country, and web of rural relationships, full of description and dialogue about the tiniest details of the characters' lives.

Cripps is waiting for a visit from Justice Overshute:

But what can look better than a kitchen, clean, and bright, and well supplied with the cheery tools of appetite. It was a good-sized room, and very picturesque with snugness. Little corners, in and out, gave play for light and shadow; the fireplace retired far enough to well express itself; and the dresser had brass-handled drawers, that seemed quietly nursing table-cloths. . . . In front of the fire sat the Carrier, with nearly all of his best clothes on, and gazing at a warming-pan. He had been forbidden to eat his supper, for fear of making a smell of it. . . . Therefore he put up his feet upon a stump of oak (which had for generations cooled down pots) and he turned with a shake of his head toward the fire, and sniffed the sniff of Tantalus. . . .

The Abingdon Arms, Beckley's venerable pub perched on the edge overlooking Otmoor. It would have seen
number of conversations from Cripps' neighbours, and has become a popular retreat from Oxford. Evelyn Waug
stayed here on his honeymoon (1928) and used it as a base for writing when he was working on *Dante Gabri
Rossetti*.

Beckley Park was the model for the house in
Aldous Huxley's *Crome Yellow*, in which the
description of a country house party and the
guests is drawn from his observations of those a
Garsington Manor.

A.E. Coppard, who wrote *Adam and Eve and Pinch Me* at Stanton St John, lived in a small cottage with the rural name Shepherd's Pit, from 1919 to 1922. He drank in the George and the Star, and played cricket for the local team in a match against neighbouring Islip. The Garsington Manor crowd came to watch.

William Cobbett's *Rural Rides* (1830) through the southern counties of England described the countryside and farming during the Enclosures of the period in a way novel to readers who had a romantic view of rural life. He did not take to the Cotswolds, which may have looked bleak and uncultivated, with sheep grazing. Like William Morris after him, he thought that the introduction of machinery was destroying the countryman's way of life, livelihood, and pride in his art and craft.

This Wold is, in itself, an ugly country. The soil is what is called a stone brash below. . . . Yet even this Wold has many fertile dells in it, and sends out, from its highest parts, several streams, each of which has its pretty valley and its meadows.

And here has come down to us, from a distance of many centuries, a particular race of sheep, called the Cotswold breed, which are of course, the best suited to the country. They are short and stocky, and appear to me to be about half way, in point of size, between the RYLANDS and the SOUTH DOWNS.

Above and opposite: Witney has long been famous for its blanket manufacturing. Cottage industry had be⟨
superseded by factories when Cobbett wrote the following:

A part, and, perhaps, a considerable part, of the decay and misery of this place, is owing to the use
machinery, and to the monopolizing, in the manufacture of Blankets, of which fabric the town of WITN⟨
(above mentioned) was the centre, and from which town the wool used to be sent round to, and the yarn,
warp, come back from, all these Cotswold villages, and quite into a part of Wiltshire. This work all now gon⟨
and so the women and the girls are a 'surplus popalashon, mon,' and are, of course, to be dealt with by t⟨
'Emigration Committee' of the Collective Wisdom! There were only a few years ago, above thirty blank⟨
manufacturers at WITNEY: twenty-five of these have been swallowed up by the five that now have all t⟨
manufacture in their hands!

Perched on the edge of the Cotswolds, Burford is known for its antique shops, old hotels and pubs, and a High Street of imposing former wool-merchants' houses. Less well known are the local quarries at Taynton which furnished stone and stone masons for buildings in Oxford. Christopher Kempster worked for Sir Christopher Wren in London, and on his own to design and build the County Hall at Abingdon.

Writers C.E. Montague, (who lived in a house built by Kempster known as Kitt's Quarries) and J.M. Falkner are buried in Burford churchyard, which contains a number of Cotswold 'woolpack'-style tombs.

Compton Mackenzie lived in a cottage on the River Windrush at the lower end of the town, and Burford was called 'Wychford' in his 1915 novel *Guy and Pauline*.

The Mitford family first moved to Asthall, near Burford in 1919, and later to Swinbrook, by the Windrush. Swinbrook House was built by their father on inherited land in 1927, to house the growing family – there were six daughters and one son. The children hated the house. On the design and directions of their father, it was austere, spartan and cold; the children's bedrooms were unheated. Diana Mitford married Sir Oswald Mosley and was a frequent visitor and friend of Lord Berners at Faringdon House, as was her sister, Nancy. Nancy Mitford (1904–73), novelist, journalist and biographer, and good friend of Evelyn Waugh, lived in Paris from 1946, came down on the socialist side of politics, and so divided the family. Her novel *The Pursuit of Love* is set in the manor at Asthall, and contains many autobiographical allusions, among them her father, Lord Merlin who was based on Lord Berners, and Merlinford, which was inspired by Faringdon House. She is buried in the churchyard.

George Orwell (whose real name was Eric Blair) left instructions that he was to be buried by the Church of England and in 'an English country churchyard'. This graveside commemoration, photographed by the *Oxford Times*, took place appropriately in Sutton Courtenay in 1984.

David Astor was a newspaper proprietor and supporter of George Orwell for many years, having employed him on the *Observer* since 1942, as well as being a personal friend. He encouraged Orwell to continue to seek a publisher for the controversial *Animal Farm*, even offering to lend him the £200 to publish it privately. As the Astors owned the manor of Sutton Courtenay, he was able to arrange Orwell's burial there, in what was certainly a perfect example of a village in the middle of 'Golden England', for which Orwell had a real emotional affinity and affection.

Sutton Courtenay village, the green, church, pub with cottages and children, everyone's ideal of a village scene.

ACKNOWLEDGEMENTS

These photographs come largely from the collections in the Centre for Oxfordshire Studies, Central Library, Westgate. In addition to acknowledging Oxfordshire County Council's Cultural Services for their use, I am indebted to Nuala La Vertue not only for her perseverance in finding all the photographs, providing photocopies to work from, and keeping them all in order, but for her knowledge of the collections, and helpful suggestions. Dr Malcolm Graham of the Centre, a walking encyclopedia of Oxfordshire and the city, has answered many questions and provided many details to add interest to the subject. Any errors of fact or omission are mine.

I would also like to thank the Vale and Downland Museum for some of the photographs illustrating the places associated with Thomas Hardy and John Betjeman: the Museum Officer John Lange and their dedicated volunteer Howard Fuller, who searched for them.

Behind the scenes are all those who have thought to donate their photographs to public collections, who I hope take pleasure in seeing them published.

The bibliography gives some further reading, and lists volumes of letters and biographies which I consulted, some compiled by the authors' relatives and descendants – I very much enjoyed their work too, in addition to the writing of the authors. I am grateful to them for making accessible the lives and private papers of their famous family members.

BIBLIOGRAPHY &
FURTHER READING

Amory, Mark: *Lord Berners, The Last Eccentric*; Chatto & Windus, 1998

Betjeman, John: *Summoned by Bells*, 1960; *Collected Poems; Church Poems*

Blackmore, R.D.: *Cripps the Carrier*, 1876

Buchan, William, ed: *John Masefield: Letters to Reyna*, 1983

Dougill, John: *Oxford in English Literature*; University of Michigan Press, 1998

Drabble, Margaret: *A Writer's Britain*, 1979

Eagle, Dorothy and Carnell, Hilary: *The Oxford Illustrated Literary Guide to Great Britain and Ireland*, OUP, 1992

Ellman, Richard: *Oscar Wilde*; Hamish Hamilton, 1987

Fitzgibbon, Constantine: *Selected Letters of Dylan Thomas*; J.M. Dent, 1966

Fothergill, J.: *An Innkeeper's Diary*, 1931

Fyvel, T.R.: *George Orwell, A Personal Memoir*; London, 1982

Hardy, Thomas: *Jude the Obscure*, 1895; paperback editions available

Hastings, Selina: *Nancy Mitford*; Hamish Hamilton, 1985

Henderson, Philip: *William Morris, His Life, Work and Friends*; Andre Deutsch, 1986

Hughes, Thomas: *Tom Brown's Schooldays; The Scouring of the White Horse; Tom Brown at Oxford*

Jerome K. Jerome: *Three Men in a Boat*; 1888, various editions

Lycett Green, Candida, ed.: *John Betjeman: Letters*: 2 vols 1926–1951; 1951–1981; Methuen, 1994 and 1995

Manley, Deborah: *Women in Oxford*, Illustrated walk by Heritage Tours, 1997

Mosley, Charlotte, ed: *Letters of Nancy Mitford*; Hodder & Stoughton, 1993

Ousby, Ian: *Literary Britain, Blue Guide*; A.C. Black, 1990

Pevsner, Nikolaus: *Oxfordshire*; Penguin, 1974

Seymour, Miranda: *Ottoline Morrell: Life on a Grand Scale*; Hodder & Stoughton, 1992

Shelden, Michael: *Orwell, The Authorised Biography*

Tames, Richard: *William Morris 1834–1896*; Shire Publications Lifelines 3, 1972

Thompson, Flora: *Lark Rise to Candleford*; 1945, Penguin

Waugh, Evelyn: *Brideshead Revisited*; 1945, Penguin